EXPLORING
CAREERS

Careers in
Mental Health

James Roland

ReferencePoint
Press®

© 2017 ReferencePoint Press, Inc.
Printed in the United States

For more information, contact:
ReferencePoint Press, Inc.
PO Box 27779
San Diego, CA 92198
www.ReferencePointPress.com

LIBRARY OF CONGRESS CATALOGING-IN-PUBLICATION DATA

Names: Roland, James. author.
Title: Careers in mental health / by James Roland.
Description: San Diego, CA : ReferencePoint Press, Inc., 2017. | Series: Exploring careers series |
    Audience: Grade 9 to 12. | Includes bibliographical references and index.
Identifiers: LCCN 2016040541 (print) | LCCN 2016041409 (ebook) | ISBN 9781682821084
    (hardback) | ISBN 9781682821091 (eBook)
Subjects: LCSH: Mental health services--Vocational guidance--Juvenile literature.
Classification: LCC RA790.75 .R65 2017 (print) | LCC RA790.75 (ebook) | DDC 616.89/023--dc23
LC record available at https://lccn.loc.gov/2016040541

Contents

A Career Focused on Helping Others

It is estimated that about one out of every five teens and adults in the United States experiences some form of mental illness in their lifetime. In any given year, between 40 million and 50 million Americans have some kind of mental disorder that could include anxiety or depression, an eating disorder, an addiction, schizophrenia, or any condition ranging from mild to serious enough to require hospitalization. "Forty-five million people in the United States have a mental illness," Richard Yep, the executive director of the American Counseling Association, said in *Pacific Standard* magazine. "I look at that and think, 'Gee, there's a lot of people that need some help.'"

While those numbers are unfortunate, they are also evidence that careers in mental health are in high demand. What is also helping make mental health care a more desirable career option are changing public attitudes about mental health. Not that long ago, seeing a psychologist or other mental health professional was viewed by many people as something to keep secret. Individuals were not always encouraged to admit they had thoughts and feelings that they did not understand or that were interfering with their daily lives.

But that is changing. More and more people look at mental health care providers in the same way they view medical doctors, dentists, occupational therapists, and other physical health care providers. "I think we're seeing a greater awareness—and also, hopefully, a destigmatization—of the importance of mental health care," Shannon Karl, associate professor in the Department of Counseling at Nova Southeastern University's College of Psychology, said in an *Orlando Sentinel* article.

Career Options

People who pursue careers in mental health have a great interest in how the human mind works. They are fascinated with how people learn, make decisions, and deal with anxiety, depression, and countless other emotions. This interest can lead to medical school and a career as a psychiatrist or to a nursing school and a career working with patients who have a mental disorder. Someone who has an interest both in human behavior and marketing could pursue a career as an advertising psychologist. Those who believe in the healing power of music, might want to consider a career as a music therapist. A passion for helping children in need could lead to a career as a child abuse counselor, school counselor, or licensed clinical social worker. The criminal justice system needs forensic psychologists to work with defendants or to help law enforcement agencies understand a crime suspect's motives. People with strong religious beliefs may combine spiritual teachings with psychology to become pastoral counselors. Mental health careers include traditional patient care in hospitals, addiction treatment clinics, and psychiatric facilities as well as corporate boardrooms, churches, schools, war zones, and just about anywhere else that comes to mind.

The educational requirements for a mental health career also vary greatly. A registered nurse specializing in psychiatry can get a job with a two-year associate's degree in nursing. A psychiatrist, on the other hand, must get a bachelor's degree and then go to medical school and earn an MD, just as a cardiologist or orthopedic surgeon must do in order to start their careers. Many jobs in mental health require a bachelor's degree and a master's degree in order to become licensed.

The encouraging news is that at the end of all that schooling, there are jobs waiting. The Bureau of Labor Statistics projects double-digit job growth for the foreseeable future in almost every area of mental health care, from psychiatrists to licensed clinical social workers to specialists in fields such as substance abuse, relationships, sports, and education.

And unlike certain careers, mental health care providers have job opportunities in all parts of the country. Unlike many high-tech jobs,

Careers in Mental Health

Clinical Psychologist	A clinical psychologist has a doctoral degree in psychology. They are trained to make diagnoses and provide individual and group therapy.
School Psychologist	A school psychologist has an advanced degree in psychology from a designated program in school psychology. They are trained to make diagnoses, provide individual and group therapy, and work with school staff to maximize efficiency in the school setting.
Clinical Social Worker	A clinical social worker is a counselor with a master's degree in social work. They are trained to make diagnoses, provide individual and group counseling, and provide case management and advocacy, many times in a hospital setting.
Mental Health Counselor	A mental health counselor has a master's degree and several years of supervised clinical work experience. They are trained to diagnose and provide individual and group counseling.
Certified Alcohol and Drug Abuse Counselor	A certified alcohol and drug abuse counselor has specific clinical training in alcohol and drug abuse. They are trained to diagnose and provide individual and group counseling.
Marital and Family Therapist	A marital and family therapist has a master's degree with special education and training in marital and family therapy. They are trained to diagnose and provide individual and group counseling.
Psychiatrist	A psychiatrist is a medical doctor with special training in the diagnosis and treatment of mental and emotional illnesses. They can prescribe medication, but they often do not counsel patients.
Psychiatric or Mental Health Nurse Practitioner	A psychiatric or mental health nurse is a registered nurse practitioner who has a master's degree and specialized training in the diagnosis and treatment of mental and emotional illness.

Source: Mental Health America, "Types of Mental Health Professionals." www.mentalhealthamerica.net.

which are concentrated in regions such as the Silicon Valley in California or certain large cities, psychiatric nurses, clinical psychologists, school psychologists, and others in this field are in demand in big cities and in rural areas, too.

Because the educational requirements can be significant and the demands of the job can be great, anyone interested in a mental health career should do some personal research. Robert Biswas-Diener, a psychology instructor at Portland State University, said in an article on the American Psychological Association website that talking to a clinical psychologist or any mental health professional about the day-to-day aspects of his or her job is helpful. "The advice I give to my own undergrads: Whichever areas you're thinking of going into, go interview a person in the field," he said.

Personal Qualities

Anyone interested in mental health careers should understand the challenges the jobs present and ask themselves if they have the qualities to pursue such careers. First and foremost, mental health workers must have a strong desire to help others, even when the patients do not understand their problems or want to accept treatment and counseling. Nurses, psychiatrists, social workers, and everyone else in the mental health field must be good communicators, able to listen and really hear what patients are telling them.

Working with those grappling with mental health disorders can often be more complicated and unpredictable than treating those with physical ailments. Unlike a broken leg or a bout of the flu, mental health conditions are often more challenging to diagnose and treat. In many cases, patients cannot clearly describe their symptoms. So being a sharp observer and having good judgment are also essential for anyone with a career in mental health. Being patient and detail oriented are also key qualities.

Finally, working in mental health often means working as part of a team. It also frequently involves the families of patients. A school psychologist, for example, needs the involvement of a student's parents to reinforce exercises and strategies covered in school sessions.

A psychiatric nurse must educate the relatives of a patient on medication about the importance of making sure the patient takes that medication as prescribed.

The challenges of helping someone with a mental health condition can be great, but the rewards can be profound. It is not for everyone, but for those with a keen interest in human emotion, behavior, and thought, the mental health field offers almost limitless opportunities and experiences.

Psychiatrist

What Does a Psychiatrist Do?

A psychiatrist treats people with mental, behavioral, and emotional disorders. But unlike most other mental health professionals, a psychiatrist can prescribe medications and order and perform a wide range of medical laboratory tests. This is because a psychiatrist has graduated from medical school and has earned an MD or DO (doctor of osteopathic medicine).

Part of a psychiatrist's approach includes talk therapy or psychotherapy. The doctor talks with patients about problems that might stem from depression, schizophrenia, bipolar disorder, or other serious mental disorders. Psychotherapy is a major part of most treatment plans for these conditions. During psychotherapy, psychiatrists listen carefully to patients describe their feelings, symptoms, and behaviors. This type of therapy also requires the psychiatrist to ask questions that will get patients to open up and think about their concerns in a new way. A patient may leave a

At a Glance:
Psychiatrist

Minimum Educational Requirements
Doctor of medicine (MD or DO)

Personal Qualities
Good listener, detail oriented, interested in how the physiology of the brain affects mental and emotional health

Certification and Licensing
Must obtain state medical license and become certified by the American Board of Psychiatry and Neurology

Working Conditions
Office setting, hospital, mental health clinic, research facility

Salary Range
About $60,000 to $200,000

Number of Jobs
About 49,000 in the United States

Future Job Outlook
Steady job growth, estimated to be about 15 percent annually through 2024

psychotherapy session with an assignment or task to approach a situation differently or talk about certain issues with family members, friends, or coworkers, and then report back on the results. Psychiatrists must also be adept at observing behaviors and picking up clues that point to the conditions affecting their patients. Psychiatrists, especially early in therapy, often interview a patient's family members to learn more about the patient's symptoms and background.

Because of their medical training, psychiatrists also look for possible physiological causes of a mental disorder. For example, are thyroid disease or low vitamin D levels making a person feel depressed? A patient's treatment, therefore, may include collaboration between a psychiatrist and another physician—either a general practitioner or a specialist. For instance, a psychiatrist may work with a cardiologist to help a patient overcome unhealthy behaviors or mental disorders such as depression to improve the patient's heart health. Research in recent years has produced evidence showing a strong connection between mental health and physical health.

A psychiatrist's ultimate goal is to find the right treatment or combination of treatments to help a patient overcome or at least manage a mental disorder. Treatments often include medications such as antidepressants or stimulants. One of the great challenges of psychiatry is finding the right combination of therapies that will make a positive difference for a patient. What works for one patient may not be right for another patient, even if the two have similar conditions. Sometimes it is a matter of trial and error to discover a treatment plan that is successful. This process can be very satisfying. "The rewards have to do with constantly being stimulated and constantly learning. Work is always challenging and not boring," Roslyn Seligman said on the College Foundation of West Virginia website. She is an associate professor of child and adolescent psychiatry at the University of Cincinnati College of Medicine. "Helping people, especially young people, is very gratifying. Seeing the sparkle in patients' eyes or seeing patients make it in life is very rewarding."

An MD or DO not only allows a psychiatrist to treat patients with medications, but also with other procedures such as electroconvulsive therapy (ECT) or deep brain stimulation (DBS). In ECT a doctor sends tiny electric currents through the brain to trigger small seizures.

A psychiatrist listens as a patient describes problems that are causing upset in her life. As a medical doctor, a psychiatrist not only listens to patients but also tries to identify possible physiological causes of mental and emotional difficulties.

The goal is to create changes in brain chemistry that will stop and reverse symptoms of certain mental conditions, such as depression or the aggression that sometimes emerges when a person has dementia. DBS also uses electricity to treat a range of conditions. In DBS tiny holes are drilled in the head and electrodes are placed on key parts of the brain. Electrical impulses are delivered to the brain to try to control symptoms of depression and Parkinson's disease.

For individuals who are interested in how brain cells and brain chemicals affect mood and mental health, psychiatry offers a lucrative and fascinating career. Psychiatrist William J. Resch, on the American Osteopathic Association website, said he believes that psychiatry requires much more individualized patient care than some fields that rely on numbers, such as blood pressure levels or cholesterol, to guide treatment. "In many other medical specialties, you treat patients algorithmically," he says. "With psychiatry, you can't do that. There is no one-size-fits-all treatment. . . . Psychiatry is tremendously intellectually stimulating, as well as challenging. I knew I would never get bored with the field."

How Do You Become a Psychiatrist?

Education

It is important to remember that psychiatry requires the greatest investment of time and the most demanding educational requirements of all mental health careers. Medical school is followed by a four-year residency, and many psychiatrists also pursue fellowships and specialty training, which extends the time before they start making "doctor money."

Because a psychiatrist must complete medical school, a strong science emphasis is recommended for an undergraduate degree. A bachelor's degree in biology or a related biological science could be helpful. A psychology degree also makes sense, especially for those who know they want to pursue psychiatry. Getting into med school requires a solid undergraduate grade point average and a good score on the Medical College Admission Test. Med school is usually a four-year program, though some universities provide an accelerated six-year undergrad/med school program for promising students.

Though an MD or DO is bestowed on graduates of med school or a college of osteopathic medicine, respectively, there is still additional training that is required. A four-year residency in psychiatry follows graduation. During residency, a new psychiatrist works in a supervised setting with patients, learning a great deal about diagnosis, treatment, and other aspects of patient care. Many psychiatrists obtain specialized education and training in university-sponsored fellowships.

Certification and Licensing

It is mandatory for psychiatrists to receive a medical license from the state in which they plan to work. Certification by the American Board of Psychiatry and Neurology is also necessary. To receive board certification, a psychiatrist must complete a training program, hold a valid state medical license, and be evaluated by board representatives who assess a psychiatrist's ability to care for patients. A psychiatrist pursuing a subspecialty, such as addiction psychiatry or geriatric psychiatry, can get certified in those areas after being licensed by the state.

Volunteer Work and Internships

Once would-be psychiatrists are in medical school, they can find internship opportunities that allow them to work in supervised clinical settings with experienced psychiatrists. Internships often include sitting in on patient assessments and consultations between psychiatrists and other health care providers. An internship in child psychiatry at the Icahn School of Medicine at Mount Sinai, for example, allows students to conduct supervised psychotherapy sessions with a variety of patients and work at an alternative high school for students who need psychiatric care or addiction treatment.

Volunteer work prior to a formal medical education may be helpful in narrowing down the specialty of psychiatry that is most appealing. In many cases, volunteer opportunities may be limited to more general mental health settings, such as a government public health office, a hospital, an addiction treatment center, or a nonprofit agency that provides counseling services. But even just becoming familiar with the world of mental health care can help focus long-term career plans.

Skills and Personality

Psychiatrists need to be very perceptive because patients with serious mental or emotional disorders may have trouble explaining their symptoms or even basic thoughts and feelings. They need to be excellent communicators, willing to listen and able to express ideas and solutions. Psychiatrists must also be very precise in ordering treatments, because the dosage of a drug, for example, can make all the difference in a patient's outcome. Psychiatrists need to be compassionate with an overriding focus on helping heal their patients. However, psychiatrists have to be careful not to let their patients' problems—some of which can be quite heartbreaking and serious—interfere with their own personal lives. Being able to separate the personal and professional parts of life is crucial for psychiatrists.

Employers

Psychiatrists work in a wide variety of employment situations. They may be in private practice, either alone or with several other mental health professionals. They may work in a hospital, drug rehabilitation clinic, research facility, prison, military setting, nursing home, university, or as part of a government or nonprofit service agency. Offices with several mental health professionals and physicians employ the highest percentage of psychiatrists, followed by psychiatric and substance abuse hospitals, outpatient care centers, general hospitals, and then government agencies, according to the Bureau of Labor Statistics (BLS).

Working Conditions

A psychiatrist may meet with patients in an office setting or in a clinical setting such as a hospital room or operating room. A psychiatrist should expect to work in a variety of locations. Psychiatrists usually have a set forty-hours-a-week schedule but may have to be on call for a certain number of nights, weekends, and holidays during the year. Psychiatrists often work with patients who are angry or unstable and must be prepared for emergencies.

On the Ross University School of Medicine website, Kendra Campbell, assistant director of the Comprehensive Psychiatric Emergency Program at New York–Presbyterian/Columbia University Medical Center, said she finds the greatest rewards working with patients in an emergency room setting. "What I like about being a psychiatrist in the emergency room is that you see people at their breaking points," she says. "I have this unique opportunity to make a profound impact on their lives. And that is a very precious, fulfilling thing."

Earnings

Like most MDs and DOs, psychiatrists tend to earn a good income. But the employment setting can make a big difference. A psychiatrist working for a community agency is going to make much less than one working in a successful private practice. Geographical differences will also affect income. The average salary for a psychiatrist is around $190,000, but it can be as low as $60,000 and well over $200,000, according to the BLS.

Opportunities for Advancement

Psychiatrists in hospital or private practice settings can move into management roles relatively quickly, as the United States faces a shortage of psychiatrists. Getting additional training and learning new skills will make a psychiatrist in private practice more valuable within that practice or as a prospect for a better position somewhere else. If research or teaching at the college level is appealing, psychiatrists can certainly angle their careers in those directions.

What Is the Future Outlook for Psychiatrists?

The medical community has expressed the need for more psychiatrists since there is a shortage, particularly in rural areas of the United States. This bodes well for individuals pursuing psychiatry as a career. Anna Ratzliff, assistant professor of psychiatry and behavioral sciences, says on the University of Washington's AIMS (Advanced Integrated Mental Health Solutions) Center website:

> One in five counties in the United States has a shortage of mental health professionals, and 96 percent of counties have a shortage of those who can prescribe medication. We help ready our residents to be active participants in the future of psychiatry—a workforce of mental health professionals able to effectively work in evidence-based, integrated care teams. There will never be enough of us, so we have to work smarter.

Find Out More

American College of Psychiatrists (ACP)
233 N. Michigan Ave., Suite 2318
Chicago, IL 60601
website: www.acpsych.org

The ACP is an honorary association that promotes the latest advances in psychiatric care and provides continuing education to its members.

American Psychiatric Association
1000 Wilson Blvd., Suite 1825
Arlington, VA 22209
website: www.psychiatry.org

The American Psychiatric Association is made up of psychiatrists working to promote the most effective treatments and care for people with mental illness. The association sponsors publications, publishes educational materials, offers career support, and generally seeks to enhance the role of psychiatry across the country.

American Psychological Association (APA)
750 First St. NE
Washington, DC 20002
website: www.apa.org

The APA promotes the development and application of psychology in all aspects of society, supports research, and advances the qualifications and standards of psychologists in a range of fields, including education.

Association of Women Psychiatrists
website: www.associationofwomenpsychiatrists.com

The organization has a twofold mission: Provide support and increase opportunities for women psychiatrists, while also raising awareness and supporting research and care of women's mental health issues.

Psychiatric Nurse

Psychiatric nurses perform a wide range of duties in treating patients with mental disorders. They also help their patients' families deal with the challenges associated with having a relative struggling with mental and emotional problems. The job is usually a mix of psychology, social work, and the kind of hands-on patient care that is common across all types of nursing. Karen McSwain, a registered psychiatric nurse, describes some of her many duties on the College Foundation of North Carolina website. "I administer medications and supervise the patient's response," she explains. "I design and run recreation programs, relaxation programs, and therapeutic interventions. I help a patient learn to cope with a panic disorder, schizophrenia, depression, grief, and mania. I work with illnesses of aging, and can differentiate between a dementia and a delirium."

In many cases a patient's first contact with mental health care is an assessment by a nurse.

At a Glance:
Psychiatric Nurse

Minimum Educational Requirements
Associate's degree

Personal Qualities
Empathy, not easily flustered, patience, good communication skills, compassion

Certification and Licensing
Must obtain a registered nurse license from state's board of nursing; can earn certification from American Nurses Credentialing Center

Working Conditions
Hospital, mental health clinic, private practice, home care

Salary Range
About $45,000 to $80,000

Number of Jobs
About 134,000 in the United States

Future Job Outlook
Steady job growth, estimated to be about 19 percent through 2022

The nurse gathers information about family history, obtains a personal mental and physical health history, discusses symptoms, and answers patient and family questions.

Depending on the setting, a psychiatric nurse can diagnose a mental illness and start a nursing treatment plan. Complex diagnoses are made by psychologists or psychiatrists, but nurses can often determine if a person is depressed, for example, and then start to work with the individual and his or her family on initial care. This might include working to make sure the patient is well hydrated (dehydration can have a major impact on mood and physical health), has a stable heart rate and blood pressure, is getting enough sleep, and is not likely to be a suicide risk or a threat to others. If those risks seem serious, the individual may need to be hospitalized temporarily. Some nurses and nurse practitioners, depending on their education and experience, can prescribe medications. Maintaining and updating patient records is also part of the job.

Once nurses gather information and make their initial diagnoses, they usually work with doctors on further aspects of care. Psychiatric nurses also assist in preparing patients for treatment. Assessing the progress of treatment and reporting that information to a psychiatrist and the patient's family is also a key part of the job. Some of this work is done independently, while in other situations it is done as part of a health care team led by a psychiatrist or neurologist.

Psychiatric nurses must also be educators. They often spend time with patients and their families, explaining a diagnosis and treatment plan. They also connect families to resources in their communities that can offer additional help. These nurses also do community outreach, informing groups about issues such as addiction, dementia, and other mental health topics.

A nurse working in a psychiatric hospital may attend to several patients during a shift, making sure medications are taken appropriately and that other aspects of care are executed properly. This includes monitoring changes in a patient and communicating changes and other important patient information to other providers during that shift, as well as those who will be working the next shift. Sometimes the job requires a nurse simply to listen to a patient and offer comforting words. At other times, a patient may become upset and aggressive. A psychiatric nurse needs to be able to calmly handle these difficult situations.

Psychiatric nurses can also specialize. Some work with children and adolescents or geriatric patients (including those with dementia). Others work with criminal offenders or people with substance abuse or eating disorder issues. Still others work with students with disabilities.

How Do You Become a Psychiatric Nurse?

Education

Psychiatric nurses must be registered nurses (RNs), which means they have at least an associate's degree. This is usually a two-year program. There are also many hospital-based nursing diploma programs that take about three years. A diploma in nursing prepares a person for an entry-level job working alongside doctors and nurses. It includes clinical training and classroom education and is often done in partnership with a local community college. Many nurses with a hospital-based diploma go on to get their associate's degree. A four-year bachelor's degree in nursing can also qualify someone to become an RN. A master's degree and even a doctorate in nursing are also options for those seeking managerial or teaching careers in this field.

Admission to nursing schools is becoming increasingly competitive, and more employers are looking for nurses with at least a bachelor's degree because they believe more education equates to better patient care. A solid high school transcript, with at least a 3.0 grade point average, and volunteer work in a health care setting will improve an applicant's chances of getting into many nursing schools. More elite colleges require a higher GPA for their nursing programs.

Nurses with more education and training can have more responsibilities, take on supervisory roles, and often make more money. A psychiatric mental health advanced practice registered nurse (PMH-APRN) has a master's or doctoral degree and can do much more in the diagnosis and treatment of a patient than a registered nurse who does not have an advanced degree. A PMH-APRN may become a nurse practitioner, which is a health care professional who has advanced training that allows her or him to treat patients without the supervision of a doctor.

Certification and Licensing

After earning a nursing degree in a two-, three-, or four-year program, candidates can take a licensing examination to become an RN. Each state's board of nursing defines the scope of responsibilities for RNs. This means that what RNs are permitted to do in one state may differ from that in a neighboring state. Certification for all psychiatric nurses is done through the American Nurses Credentialing Center (ANCC). At least thirty hours of continuing education in psychiatric nursing and two thousand hours of clinical practice in psychiatric nursing are required to earn ANCC psychiatric nursing certification.

Volunteer Work and Internships

Volunteer work and internships are important in preparing for a career as a psychiatric nurse. Volunteering at a hospital, health care agency, or community organization that works with people with mental disorders is a good way to decide whether psychiatric nursing is a good fit.

Skills and Personality

One of the most valuable qualities a psychiatric nurse must possess in compassion. "Those who work with the mentally ill have a deep and abiding respect for people—you have to have compassion and concern to work with people in psychic pain," said Linda K. Tuyn, an assistant professor with the Decker School of Nursing, on the *Binghamton University Magazine* website. "It is humbling and potentially spiritually broadening and helps you to learn about and be in touch with your real self."

Time management is also essential, particularly for psychiatric nurses who work at a hospital or clinic and are responsible for several patients during their shift. Some patients may require talk therapy from a nurse, while others need medications. Nurses also consult with doctors about patients during a shift or prepare patients for procedures. Making sure each patient gets enough attention and the proper care can be a real challenge.

Unlike many other nursing situations, treating patients with mental disorders can be quite unpredictable. A patient may be calm one moment and hostile and aggressive the next. A psychiatric nurse needs to able to use good judgment about how to respond in situations like this. Good communication skills are essential.

On the Job

Employers

Psychiatric nurses work in a variety of settings including psychiatric hospitals, medical offices, mental health centers, or drug rehabilitation clinics. They may work for community organizations that help the mentally ill and educate citizens about mental illness. These nurses are also employed in school districts and correctional facilities. They are also employed by home health care agencies.

Working Conditions

Like other nursing specialties, psychiatric nursing is a demanding job that keeps nurses on their feet and moving fast. In some settings, a psychiatric nurse has time to get to know patients and their families. In other situations, though, the job is more about making sure patients are receiving their proper treatment. Psychiatric nurses often encounter patients during a crisis, such as a suicide attempt or after a domestic violence incident. Nurses in a hospital setting will deal with a variety of patients and mental disorders every day. In some locations, restraining a patient is necessary, though more often it is a matter of defusing a potential confrontation. Nurses who work in a facility for older adults with dementia may have to help with hygiene and dressing concerns, as well as recreational and therapeutic services. Home health care nurses do most of their work in a patient's home or by accompanying a patient to a doctor's appointment or other destination.

Earnings

The average annual salary for a psychiatric nurse is about $57,000, and the range is about $45,000 to $79,000, according to PayScale.

com. Nurses with an associate's degree make less than those with a bachelor's or master's degree. Nurses who are in supervisory roles tend to make more than those who are not part of the management team at a facility.

Opportunities for Advancement

Advancement for psychiatric nurses depends largely on their education and training. Getting a master's or a doctorate and becoming a PMH-APRN is the surest way to move up to a managerial role. A nursing supervisor in a large facility, for example, is an important member of the senior management team. There are opportunities and needs for nurses at all levels throughout the world.

Psychiatric nurses who want to advance their educations and career opportunities can earn a master's degree or doctorate and become nurse practitioners (NPs). They can do much more than RNs in terms of diagnosing and treating patients. NPs also focus on prevention and health management. An NP who has specialized in psychiatric care can become a consultation/liaison. A consultation/liaison nurse practitioner is the psychiatric expert advising the medical staff at a hospital. These professionals work at the intersection of mental and physical health.

What Is the Future Outlook for Psychiatric Nurses?

Job growth in this field is expected to be double digits for the foreseeable future. There are needs for these nurses in all regions of the country. Rural areas in particular face shortages of well-trained psychiatric nurses. "We are in a dire need to increase the supply of mental health care providers and increase access to care for individuals and families with mental health needs," said Jeannette Andrews, dean for the College of Nursing at the University of South Carolina, on the College of Nursing's website.

Mental health is an aspect of medicine in which new discoveries and treatments are being developed every year. As a nurse in this area, you can be right in the middle of an exciting and rewarding field.

Find Out More

American Psychiatric Association
1000 Wilson Blvd., Suite 1825
Arlington, VA 22209
website: www.psychiatry.org

The American Psychiatric Association is made up of psychiatrists working to promote the most effective treatments and care for people with mental illness. The association sponsors publications, publishes educational materials, offers career support, and generally seeks to enhance the role of psychiatry across the country.

American Psychiatric Nurses Association (APNA)
3141 Fairview Park Dr., Suite 625
Falls Church, VA 22042
website: www.apna.org

The APNA provides information and support for nurses already in the field, as well as for anyone interesting in pursuing the career. The association sponsors continuing education programs and shares information about the latest news and practices affecting psychiatric nursing care.

International Society of Psychiatric-Mental Health Nurses
2424 American Ln.
Madison, WI 53704
website: www.ispn-psych.org

The organization promotes psychiatric-mental health nursing around the world and fosters communication between these nurses and educators in the field. The association is active with projects such as scholarships for nursing students and conferences for psychiatric-mental health nurses and related occupations.

National Student Nurses Association (NSNA)
website: www.nsna.org

The NSNA provides educational support and career resources for individuals considering a nursing career, as well as those currently seeking a diploma. The website is a helpful resource whether you are considering psychiatric nursing or any nursing specialty.

Clinical Psychologist

Clinical psychologists have some of the most wide-ranging jobs in mental health. They can treat patients across a wide spectrum of conditions, from mild anxiety to obsessive-compulsive disorder. They can work with children, teens, and adults. Clinical psychologists help children with Asperger's syndrome, teens with bulimia, veterans with post-traumatic stress disorder, and older adults coping with depression after losing a spouse.

Psychologists may choose to specialize in fields such as child psychology, rehabilitation psychology, industrial and workplace psychology, forensic psychology, and even sleep psychology. Or a psychologist may focus on research, studying the effectiveness of various interventions, such as cognitive behavior therapy, on different populations. Clinical psychologists also work with government agencies, helping create policies for dealing with mental illness. "In clinical psychology, one can teach at

At a Glance:
Clinical Psychologist

Minimum Educational Requirements

Master's degree but most obtain doctorates

Personal Qualities

Problem solver, good communicator, comfortable working with all ages and types of people

Certification and Licensing

Must obtain license from a state licensing agency; many obtain board certification

Working Conditions

Mostly indoors in hospital, clinic, and office settings

Salary Range

About $46,000 to $107,000, higher if self-employed

Number of Jobs

As of 2015, about 173,000 in the United States

Future Job Outlook

Steady job growth, estimated to be about 19 percent through 2022 all sorts of levels, do research, work in business, at hospitals, engage in clinical work and more," Yale University psychology professor Alan E. Kadzin said in an article on the American Psychological Association (APA) website. "What career flexibility!"

Clinical psychologists must have a strong understanding of the many factors that can cause a mental disorder (chemical imbalance, childhood trauma, and so on) and knowledge of how disorders can be diagnosed. They also need to be familiar with possible interventions and treatments for a variety of mental and emotional conditions. Unlike psychiatrists, who can prescribe medications and oversee certain invasive treatments such as electroconvulsive therapy, psychologists are not medical doctors. This means they cannot prescribe medications or certain treatments. But a clinical psychologist still has a broad range of therapies that can be used to help patients.

A clinical psychologist helps patients with emotional, intellectual, social, and behavioral challenges. The process usually begins with a patient filling out paperwork describing his or her personal and family history of physical and mental health. The patient is then asked to describe any mental or emotional concerns. From there, a clinical psychologist begins to assess the patient and diagnose any mental disorders that may be present. This is usually done in conversations in which the psychologist asks the patient to talk about himself or herself. At some point the conversation usually turns to the issues that brought the patient there in the first place.

Clinical psychology is rooted in psychotherapy, or talk therapy. A psychologist listens to a patient talk about feelings, thoughts, fears, behaviors, and memories, and then comes up with a diagnosis. Sometimes a preliminary diagnosis is made during the first appointment. Other times it takes several appointments to pin down the real problem, especially if a patient is not forthcoming. Psychotherapy is about much more than diagnosing a mental disorder. It is usually at the heart of treatment. "Hundreds of studies have found that psychotherapy is an effective way to help people make positive changes in their lives," says Katherine C. Nordal, the APA's executive director for professional practice, in an article on the APA's website. "Compared with medication, psychotherapy has fewer side effects and lower instances of relapse when discontinued."

As the sessions go along, a psychologist gives the patient strategies or tools to help confront his or her problems. At the end of each appointment, a clinical psychologist may give the patient homework. It could be something as simple as writing down the details of moments the patient felt anxious. Or it might be a more difficult assignment, such as confronting a relative about a lingering family issue or deliberately fighting an urge to smoke a cigarette or engage in a compulsive behavior.

During these sessions, the clinical psychologist might see a need to involve other specialists or agencies. Clinical psychologists often work with mental and physical health care providers, as well as social service agencies, to come up with the best treatment plan. For example, an older adult who has become depressed because she cannot drive may get a psychological boost from therapy as well as the assistance of a senior service agency that offers transportation.

In many cases, a clinical psychologist will work with patients for a period of months or even years with the ultimate goal of helping them overcome their challenges or at least have the tools to deal with their issues on their own. Clinical psychologist John Duffy said in an article on Psych Central:

> There are a few reasons I love being a psychotherapist. First, I find it to be a singular honor and privilege to play a part in the stories of my clients. Also, I cannot think of a more rewarding career, one that is designed solely to decrease suffering and improve quality of life. Finally, I celebrate those moments where I see hope in the eyes of a client, or a recognition of her own greatness, or a long-abandoned hearty laugh. There's nothing I'd rather do with my life. I consider myself so lucky to do this job.

How Do You Become a Clinical Psychologist?

Education

Clinical psychologists usually get a bachelor's degree in psychology or a related field such as counseling, behavioral science, or gerontology.

A master's or doctoral program may take someone with a bachelor's degree in a subject other than psychology, but generally, an undergraduate degree in psychology is the best way to start.

A master's degree in psychology can be enough to obtain a clinical psychologist's license. However, to work independently as a clinical psychologist, most states require a doctorate, which usually takes four to seven years to complete. Without a doctoral degree, a clinical psychologist can work in many other settings, though it is usually done with the supervision of a clinical psychologist holding a doctorate.

Certification and Licensing

Each state has a licensing board that reviews an applicant's education and work/internship experience before granting a license. The APA recommends two thousand hours of clinical service during internships and two thousand hours of supervised clinical service after earning a degree. The exact number of hours required by each state's licensing board differs from state to state.

Clinical psychology certification is available through the American Board of Professional Psychology. The certification process includes a review of an applicant's educational and professional credentials, as well as a peer-reviewed practice sample. A practice sample includes several elements, such as a list of published research articles, a detailed statement about the applicant's education and career, and reports from cases on which he or she has worked. An oral examination is also required. In certain specialties, a written exam may also be necessary.

Volunteer Work and Internships

Community-based mental health or social service agencies often welcome volunteer assistance. While direct patient care or research opportunities may be limited due to patient privacy issues, simply being around this type of work may help interested individuals decide whether or not to pursue a career in psychology.

At the undergraduate level, many universities have internship programs for psychology students. The APA maintains an excellent list of opportunities in schools and organizations across the country. For students in master's or doctoral programs, internships are essential in earning the degrees. The Association of Psychology Postdoctoral and Internship Centers keeps a directory of university-based public and private programs for students and recent graduates.

Skills and Personality

Clinical psychologists need to be good listeners but also keen observers of body language and their patients' choice of words. They need to know how to ask the right questions to get patients to open up. They also need to have good judgment that will guide them in making the right treatment decisions for their patients. It is essential that they be detail oriented, empathetic, and patient and have a great interest in how the mind works. Because they are dealing with patients who are having problems, clinical psychologists should have an even-keeled personality that keeps them from getting flustered and keeps their patients calm and focused on dealing with their issues.

Bruce Wampold, a professor of psychology at the University of Wisconsin–Madison, says in an article on the APA website that flexibility is vital for a psychologist. This is because a psychologist must deal with all kinds of people and a wide range of mental disorders. "Successful therapists or effective therapists are able to form a working relationship with a variety of patients," he says. He adds that a dedication to improving the craft is another of the most important qualities a clinical psychologist should possess: "Effective therapists seem to be those who are reflective and practice deliberately to get better."

On the Job

Employers

Clinical psychologists are employed by a wide array of organizations. They work in traditional hospitals, mental health facilities, schools, universities, the military, the criminal justice system, the government, and various business and industries. Clinical psychologists are found in large practices that include many other mental health professionals. Many psychologists also go into private practice for themselves. This can be a great challenge but also more lucrative than many other workplace situations.

Working Conditions

Generally, clinical psychologists work in an office or hospital-like setting. They may work with clients in a comfortable office that helps patients relax. But they also may see patients in a more clinical setting, such as a hospital, rehabilitation center, or mental health clinic. They might see children and families in school or see criminal defendants in a correctional institution.

The working conditions can be somewhat unpredictable, as some people with mental disorders display erratic behavior. They may become upset and cry or become angry and lash out. But most of the time, clinical psychologists are able to maintain a calm and peaceful environment. Clinical psychologists who see patients regularly often work evenings or weekends to accommodate their patients' schedules.

Earnings

The median salary for a clinical psychologist in 2015 was $72,580, according to the Bureau of Labor Statistics. The range of salaries was about $46,000 to around $107,000. The wide salary range depends primarily on education, work experience, location, and employer. A psychologist with a PhD can earn more than one with a master's degree, for instance. Working in a large metropolitan area usually pays more than a similar job in a rural area. Clinical psychologists with their own practices could earn more than $200,000 annually.

Opportunities for Advancement

A clinical psychologist with a master's degree can make more money and move into a managerial role in a practice or hospital by earning a doctorate. Psychologists with a doctorate have more promising long-term job prospects and more options than those without. Because clinical psychologists are employed in so many different settings, there are always job openings for those with the right experience. However, specializing in a particular field may improve prospects, because there are fewer specialists in the job pool than those with a general clinical psychology background.

What Is the Future Outlook for Clinical Psychologists?

There were about 173,000 clinical psychologists employed throughout the United States in 2015, but that number is expected to increase by about 19 percent during the next decade. Because the stigma is lifting on mental health, and more people in industry, education, and government are recognizing the benefits of therapy, clinical psychologists should have not only more job prospects in the future, but greater appreciation for their efforts, too.

Find Out More

American Academy of Clinical Psychology (AACPSY)
211 E. Davis Blvd.
Tampa, FL 33606
website: www.aacpsy.org

The AACPSY fosters greater communication between member psychologists, provides mentors for people preparing to enter the field, and works to advance the understanding of clinical psychology in the general public.

American Psychological Association (APA)
750 First St. NE
Washington, DC 20002
website: www.apa.org

The APA promotes the development and application of psychology in all aspects of society, supports research, and advances the qualifications and standards of psychologists in a range of fields, including education.

Association for Psychological Science
1800 Massachusetts Ave. NW, Suite 402
Washington, DC 20036
website: www.psychologicalscience.org

The organization promotes science-based psychological research and practices. It provides mentors, grants, and employment assistance for students, as well as support for researchers investigating psychological science. It also publishes journals that provide a platform for researchers to share their work.

Society of Clinical Psychology
website: www.div12.org

This division of the American Psychological Association focuses on the integration of clinical psychology in education, research, practice, and public policy. The Society of Clinical Psychology is also an excellent resource for information on various mental disorders and the most effective treatments, as well as career information.

School Psychologist

A school psychologist's primary goal is to help students be successful in school—not just academically, but emotionally and socially, too. A school psychologist must understand how a student's emotional, mental, behavioral, and social development affects the ability to learn. A few of the many issues a school psychologist confronts are students with depression, attention-deficit/hyperactivity disorder, learning disabilities, and challenges related to language barriers, gender identity, and family problems. "There's a direct correlation between emotional health and academic success," says Susan Swearer, a professor of school psychology at the University of Nebraska–Lincoln, in the online edition of *Monitor on Psychology*.

A school psychologist typically has a strong background in psychology and education, including a solid understanding of different student learning styles and how different school or classroom environments can affect

At a Glance:

School Psychologist

Minimum Educational Requirements

Master's degree

Personal Qualities

Empathetic, likes to solve problems, good communicator, comfortable working with children

Certification and Licensing

Must obtain credential from a state educational agency

Working Conditions

Mostly indoors, in school and office settings

Salary Range

About $41,000 to $117,000

Number of Jobs

As of 2015, about 105,000 in the United States

Future Job Outlook

Steady job growth, estimated to be 11 percent through 2022

the way students behave and learn. In the same *Monitor on Psychology* article, Frank C. Worrell, director of the school psychology program at the University of California–Berkeley, says a school psychologist stands at the intersection of psychological treatment and classroom achievement. "It's a combination specialty," he says. "The solution to a psychology problem may be an academic intervention, and the solution to an academic problem may be a psychological intervention. Recognizing the connection between these worlds is important."

School psychologists work with students individually, as well as with teachers and administrators on school-wide programs and policies. One day a school psychologist may work one-on-one with a student, diagnosing a learning disability and coming up with an Individual Education Plan that provides specific classroom strategies to help that student succeed. The next day that same school psychologist might work with counselors, teachers, and other school officials on an antibullying program. The week may also include testing students to determine placement in gifted or special needs programs, meeting with parents to discuss the academic and social needs of their children, helping teachers deal with classroom discipline problems, working with students at risk of dropping out, and a wide variety of other tasks and responsibilities.

It is a demanding job but one that can have many rewards. In the Fall 2015 issue of Lewis and Clark College's *Chronicle*, New Hampshire's School Psychologist of the Year Kate Grieve describes the most satisfying parts of the job:

> I love the diverse nature of my work—the opportunity to collaborate and strategize with colleagues, to intervene and educate young people in ways that create meaningful change. . . . My favorite part of the day is working one-on-one with students in my office. I explain what tests reveal about their individual learning styles, including their strengths and weaknesses. We focus on solutions, not problems.

The responsibilities of a school psychologist occasionally overlap with those of a school counselor. But the two jobs differ in some important areas. School psychologists usually work more with students who have identified special needs, such as learning disabilities or mental health conditions like depression, anxiety, or substance abuse. Counselors deal with a school's general population. They might help students work through issues related to peer pressure, for example. At the high school level, counselors are often more involved in helping with course selection and postgraduation career planning.

How Do You Become a School Psychologist?

Education

High school students interested in becoming a school psychologist may want to talk with the psychologist assigned to their school to learn more about what the job entails. Those students may also want to take a psychology course at their school if one is available.

Most school psychologists begin their studies by earning a bachelor's degree in educational psychology, general psychology, counseling psychology, or a related subject such as education, sociology, or child development. They then move on to course work toward a master's degree or a specialist's degree in school psychology. A specialist's degree usually requires at least sixty hours of course work, which is more than most master's programs, but does not require a thesis (as most master's degree programs do). Most states require a specialist's degree and/or a doctorate in school psychology (at least ninety hours of postgraduate work) to license someone as a school psychologist. Internships are also required. Once a school psychologist is licensed, continuing education is required to maintain a license and to keep up-to-date with the latest in research and practices in the field.

Certification and Licensing

Each state educational agency (SEA) has slightly different requirements for obtaining a credential to work in a public school setting. At a minimum, these usually include a master's or specialist's degree and a certain number of hours in an internship. Some testing may also be required by the SEA.

To obtain a license as a clinical psychologist, the American Psychological Association recommends two thousand hours of clinical service during internships and two thousand hours of clinical service after earning a degree. However, the number of hours needed to secure a school psychologist license differs from one state to the next.

The National Association of School Psychologists (NASP) will issue the Nationally Certified School Psychologist credential to professionals who meet a stringent set of requirements involving testing and work experience. The designation reflects high standards of professionalism and is used by many states to satisfy their requirements for a licensed school psychologist credential.

Volunteer Work and Internships

Getting volunteer or internship experience in school psychology can be tricky in high school because much of the work with individual students is confidential. But high school students may be able to work on school-wide or district-wide programs on self-esteem or other topics that do not involve individual student records.

Getting volunteer and internship experience as an undergraduate can also help educate students about a career in educational psychology. While earning a master's degree or a doctorate, a yearlong internship—at least twelve hundred hours—is usually required.

The NASP has guidelines for internships that involve assessment, consultation, counseling, intervention, prevention, and other subjects. School districts that provide internship opportunities usually let college students rotate through several K–12 school and administrative settings. Part of the internship might include work with elementary school students, with another rotation at a high school or perhaps the school district headquarters.

Skills and Personality

Communication skills are essential for a school psychologist. He or she frequently shares information with and takes input from classroom teachers, school counselors, and mental health care providers working with students outside the school setting. Another key part of a school psychologist's job is communicating with a student's family about what can be done at home to reinforce strategies and behaviors taught at school. The school psychologist may be the first school

A school psychologist works with a student. These mental health professionals perform a variety of tasks, including testing for learning disabilities and developing individualized education plans for those students, helping teachers with classroom discipline problems, and working with students at risk of dropping out.

representative to inform parents about a student's learning disability, behavior problem, or other issue. "Sometimes you have to tell parents what they don't want to hear," says Phoenix elementary school psychologist Mike Junge on the Mississippi Department of Education's career planning website. "But you can present bad news in a way so parents feel comfortable."

Empathy—the ability to put oneself in someone else's shoes and understand what that person is feeling—is also important. This can be especially challenging when working with young students, who may not be able to communicate their feelings clearly or may be uncomfortable discussing personal and sensitive issues with a stranger.

School psychologists must also be very organized. They work with a lot of students, teachers, and administrators on a multitude of issues. Multitasking is a big part of the job, because it involves assessments, interventions, counseling, data analysis, meetings, report writing, and other responsibilities.

Employers

Most school psychologists are employed by public school districts or private schools. School psychologists are also employed in universities, the juvenile justice system, hospitals, treatment centers, and private practice, where they may contract with schools. Those employed by universities may be there doing research or teaching. Or they may be helping college students with issues such as time management, stress reduction, and substance abuse.

School districts should employ one school psychologist for every five hundred to seven hundred students, according to NASP guidelines. But that ratio varies greatly among districts and states, usually as a result of budget demands and the priorities of the school district.

Working Conditions

Most work by school psychologists is done in an office or conference room setting, as well as in the classroom. In many school districts, psychologists have to travel to different schools and to the district's headquarters for meetings, training, and other reasons.

School psychologists working for a public school district will usually follow the same work calendar as the school system. That often means having summers off.

Earnings

The median salary for a school psychologist in 2015 was $76,040, according to the Bureau of Labor Statistics. The range of salaries was about $41,000 to around $117,000. The wide salary range depends primarily on education, work experience, and the cost of the living in that school district.

Opportunities for Advancement

A school psychologist with a master's degree or specialist's degree can make more money and take on more supervisory roles by earning a doctorate. A school-based psychologist may be able to move up to the school district's centralized departments of mental health services or behavioral services. This would be more of an administrative job, with less time spent counseling individual students. But it would provide the opportunity to help shape the services and programs offered by the school district.

What Is the Future Outlook for School Psychologists?

There were about 105,000 school psychologists employed throughout the United States in 2015, but that number was expected to increase steadily. That is because the demand for school psychologists is growing, according to the Bureau of Labor Statistics. In 2012 the agency declared school psychologists among the five fastest-growing career options for individuals with doctoral degrees. "We simply haven't been able to turn out enough people to fill available jobs," LeAdelle Phelps, associate dean for academic affairs at the State University of New York–Buffalo and chair of the Council of Directors of School Psychology Programs, reported on the American Psychological Association website.

A growing awareness of how a student's mental and emotional health affects success in school is helping fuel job growth in school psychology. "School board members, parents and the community are now telling schools to pay more attention to mental health," says Ron Palomares, the American Psychological Association's assistant executive director for policy and advocacy in the schools.

That is encouraging news to individuals with an interest in school psychology and a desire to help children reach their potential. Phelps notes: "You have a tremendous opportunity to provide early preventative services to children and make a significant difference in their lives."

Find Out More

American Board of School Psychology
600 Market St., Suite 201
Chapel Hill, NC 27516
website: www.abpp.org

One of the member boards of the American Board of Professional Psychology, the American Board of School Psychology helps establish the criteria and requirements for training, education, and competencies related to board certification in school psychology.

American Psychological Association (APA)
750 First St. NE
Washington, DC 20002
website: www.apa.org

The APA promotes the development and application of psychology in all aspects of society, supports research, and advances the qualifications and standards of psychologists in a range of fields, including education.

International School Psychology Association (ISPA)
Leidseplein 5, 1017 PR Amsterdam
Netherlands
website: www.ispaweb.org

The ISPA promotes greater communication and sharing of practices and research among school psychologists around the world. The group also advocates for expanded use of school psychologists in regions where these jobs do not exist.

National Association of School Psychologists (NASP)
4340 East West Highway, Suite 402
Bethesda, MD 20814
website: www.nasponline.org

The NASP is the largest organization of school psychologists. It seeks to advance the practices of school psychologists as they relate to the improvement of student academic achievement, behavior, and mental health.

Sports Psychologist

An athlete may be in top physical condition and a master of the skills required for his or her chosen sport. But that same athlete may also have trouble focusing during a game or may let the pressure of a big moment become too overwhelming. Communication with teammates or coaches might be a problem. Whatever the reason, the athlete's mental approach needs attention.

That is where a sports psychologist comes in. These mental health professionals are specially trained to help athletes overcome the mental and emotional challenges that keep them from performing their best on the field, court, rink, or wherever they compete. Sports psychology is sometimes referred to as performance psychology, because the field can include work with dancers and other nonsports performers. "Many athletes feel their success in sports is due to mental factors and psychological mastery," says

At a Glance:

Sports Psychologist

Minimum Educational Requirements

Doctoral degree

Personal Qualities

Interested in sports and performance, good listener, motivator, flexible

Certification and Licensing

Must obtain credential from a state educational agency, can be board certified in sports and/or performance psychology

Working Conditions

Office or clinical setting, athletic training facilities

Salary Range

About $60,000 to $120,000

Number of Jobs

About 200 in the United States

Future Job Outlook

Steady job growth, estimated to be about 11 percent annually through 2022

Shilagh Mirgain, a sports psychologist with the University of Wisconsin School of Medicine and Public Health on the school's News and Events website. "They may have physically trained well, but how they show up on the day of competition and manage their mental focus can determine the outcome of that performance."

A sports psychologist is usually a person with a strong interest in sports or exercise but is also fascinated with how mental health intersects with physical performance. Professional sports teams, university athletic departments, and individual athletes hire sports psychologists to help athletes maximize their potential. A sports psychologist might use visualization techniques to help an athlete overcome an obstacle or mental block. This could involve teaching a basketball player relaxation techniques that allow the athlete to picture himself or herself sinking a free throw. The same approach might be used to help a golfer stay calm over a big putt or a gymnast relax on the balance beam.

Major League Baseball catcher Jarrod Saltalamacchia turned to a sports psychologist when he was having trouble simply throwing the ball back to the pitcher. He had suffered a shoulder injury and then had surgery, but his problem was both physical and mental. He learned a technique to keep him from focusing on the discomfort in his shoulder. But he had to get past the stigma of asking a psychologist for help, according to an article on ESPN.com. "You don't want anyone to know you're getting help," he says. "But you're getting help in the training room, why not get help for other issues? It's done wonders for me."

Sports psychologists must know a variety of therapies and strategies to help athletes deal a wide range of challenges. One common approach that a sports psychologist uses is to teach athletes positive self-talk, which is essentially training the inner voice to focus on encouraging and constructive messages. A sports psychologist must also be able to teach breathing exercises that enhance relaxation and focus. Sports psychologists help teach experienced athletes as well as young people to handle pressure from coaches, fans, and even parents. A sports psychologist may also help an athlete stay on a training regimen by finding ways to motivate that individual. "Everyone is trying to figure out how to maximize talent," says Scott Goldman, director of clinical and sports psychology at the University of Arizona, on the

American Psychological Association (APA) website. Sports psychologists can help athletes reach their potential.

One of the toughest challenges facing any athlete is recovering from an injury. Athletes might doubt they can fully recover. They might worry about getting hurt again. Good sports psychologists can help them find ways to mentally cope with the pain or overcome fears and doubts to stay on track during recovery.

There are also situations in which a sports psychologist works with an entire team or within a program such as a university's athletic department. At least twenty American universities have a sports psychologist on staff, while dozens more contract with private sports psychologists. Their challenge is not just to help student athletes perform better in their sports, but in the classroom, too, and in all aspects of college environment. "It's not just for performance, but to make sure that student athletes are well-rounded," says Gloria Balague, a psychology professor at the University of Illinois–Chicago on the APA website.

Sports psychologists will often work one-on-one with an athlete. They may also hold workshops or meet with athletes, trainers, and coaches in groups to help them learn how to communicate and cooperate better, deal with team conflicts, and handle any other types of adversity as a team.

If an athlete who works with a sports psychologist is successful, then that mental health professional will have an extra reason to cheer that touchdown or gold medal or simply that comeback an athlete makes after getting hurt. "It's really rewarding to be part of this and watch the athletes shine after all the hard work they've done," Charlie Brown, a sports psychologist who has worked with Olympians, said on the APA website.

How Do You Become a Sports Psychologist?

Education

Most sports psychologists begin their formal education with a bachelor's degree in psychology, though some start out with degrees in exercise science, kinesiology, or some other sports-related subject.

There are some undergraduate programs specific to sports psychology. Some universities offer master's degrees in sports and performance psychology. But a doctorate in psychology is still necessary to become a licensed psychologist.

There are opportunities to earn a PhD that focuses on sports psychology. Oregon State University, for example, offers a PhD in exercise and sports science with a concentration in sports psychology. The University of North Texas offers a similar PhD program. These and other similar PhD programs typically take four years to complete after earning a bachelor's degree. The APA recognizes a proficiency in sports psychology only as a postgraduate focus after one has earned a doctorate in psychology and been licensed as a psychologist. At that point, a psychologist can specialize in courses and training focused on sports and performance psychology.

Certification and Licensing

The APA suggests getting two thousand hours of clinical service during internships and two thousand hours of clinical service after obtaining a PhD in order to qualify for a license as a clinical psychologist. Each state has slightly different licensing requirements.

There are no specific sports or performance-related requirements a psychologist needs to start working in that field. However, someone who wants to specialize in sports psychology should take the courses and get whatever training is possible to establish some credentials as an expert in sports psychology.

A sports psychologist can become certified by the American Board of Sport Psychology (ABSP). To obtain certification, a sports psychologist must complete a long list of board-approved modules, a final project, and work on a prescribed number of athlete assessments and intervention consultations.

Internships

Because sports psychology is a relatively new field, a would-be sports psychologist may have a harder time finding an internship or work experience in that specialty compared to general psychology. But getting experience working with athletes and teams early on can be a huge help in giving a career a head start.

The APA's Exercise and Sport Psychology Division and the ABSP have resources available to help sports psychologists find internships and supervised clinical experience. Universities that offer sports and performance degrees may also be able to help students and graduates find opportunities in sports psychology. Another helpful organization is the AASP, which also provides certification and helps promote training and education in the field of sports psychology.

Skills and Personality

Sports psychologists do not need to be great athletes, but they do need to be knowledgeable about the challenges athletes face. An interest in sports and performance is necessary. It is also helpful to have a solid understanding of exercise science, anatomy, and athletic training.

Like any group of people, athletes include a mix of personalities. Not surprisingly, they tend to be more competitive than the average person, and they may be unrealistic about how far they can take their skills and talents. That is why a good sports psychologist must be enthusiastic and a good motivator, while also being able to help people see their limitations along with their strengths.

Sports psychologists must also be good listeners, able to identify the mental blocks that may keep an athlete from optimal performance. And sports psychologists should be comfortable working alongside trainers and coaches as part of a team.

On the Job

Employers

Sports psychologists are often self-employed professionals who work with an individual athlete or who contract with a professional team or university. But many sports psychologists are also hired as full-time employees of a university athletic department or a professional sports team. Sports psychologists also work in counseling centers and sports medicine clinics.

Working Conditions

A sports psychologist works with clients in an office setting and at an athlete's training facility. The nature of the athlete's challenges will dictate the setting. That basketball player struggling to make free throws may work with a sports psychologist in the gym on relaxation and concentration techniques, for example.

Earnings

Psychologists, in general, make an average of about $90,000 a year, with some making as much as $120,000 or more, according to the Bureau of Labor and Statistics. Sports psychologists can expect to make around the same. The APA says that sports psychologists employed by universities can expect to earn between $60,000 and $80,000, with some topping six figures.

Opportunities for Advancement

A sports psychologist in private practice can advance by building a larger client base and working with more high-profile athletes. A sports psychologist who becomes part of the staff at a sports medicine clinic or other institution can advance into managerial roles with time. If employed by a university, advancement could occur at that institution or by moving up to a bigger university. "Oddly enough, many athletic departments struggle to find a number of qualified candidates that have experience in both clinical issues and working with athletes," Brent Walker, associate athletics director for Championship Performance at Columbia University and president of the Association for Applied Sport Psychology, said in an e-mail interview. "Therefore, the field faces a dilemma in that the future may hold more positions than qualified candidates."

What Is the Future Outlook for Sports Psychologists?

Sports is a multibillion-dollar industry that shows no sign of shrinking. The role of sports psychologists is likely to grow in the years ahead, as more athletes, coaches, and others involved with sports see the value of giving proper attention to the mental and emotional aspects of performance and competition.

It is a growing field for individuals with a passion for sports and psychology. "We found that [National Collegiate Athletic Association] collegiate athletes and coaches are highly receptive to the addition of mental skills training and performance consulting," says Craig Wrisberg, professor of sports psychology at the University of Tennessee, on the Association for Applied Sport Psychology website. "The field is headed toward a level of acceptance that will be evidenced by the addition of staff in the field of sport and exercise psychology to public and private organizations that seek to provide participants with the highest-quality experiences."

Find Out More

American Board of Sport Psychology
website: www.americanboardofsportpsychology.org

This organization seeks to advance education and training in sports psychology. It offers certification to sports psychologists who meet the necessary educational and work experience requirements and who participate in board-approved continuing education.

American Psychological Association (APA)
750 First St. NE
Washington, DC 20002
website: www.apa.org

The APA promotes the development and application of psychology in all aspects of society, supports research, and advances the qualifications and standards of psychologists in a range of fields, including education.

Association for Applied Sport Psychology (AASP)
8365 Keystone Crossing, Suite 107
Indianapolis, IN 46240
website: www.appliedsportpsych.org

The AASP shares relevant news and research about sports psychology and promotes the benefits of sports psychologists in the world of professional and amateur sports and fitness. The organization also promotes networking and greater communication among sports psychologists around the United States.

International Society of Sport Psychology (ISSP)
website: www.issponline.org

The ISSP promotes the practice and advancement of sports psychology worldwide and encourages more research in the field. The organization brings together experts for conferences around the world, helping improve the practice of sports and performance psychology and the profile of this unique psychological discipline.

Marriage and Family Therapist

What Does a Marriage and Family Therapist Do?

At a Glance:

Marriage and Family Therapist

Minimum Educational Requirements

Master's degree

Personal Qualities

Empathetic, ability to see both sides, comfortable working with couples and children

Certification and Licensing

Must obtain license from a state licensing agency

Working Conditions

Usually in an office setting at a clinic, hospital, or therapist's office

Salary Range

About $31,000 to $82,000

Number of Jobs

As of 2015, about 48,000 in the United States

Future Job Outlook

Steady job growth, estimated to be 19 percent through 2024

When a couple faces a relationship problem or parents are at odds with their children or a family faces some type of crisis, they can turn to a marriage and family therapist for help. Marriage and family therapy (MFT) helps couples identify problems within their relationship or those affecting their relationship from the outside, and works with the couple on strategies to help overcome them. A family therapist may do the same kind of work when the relationship is between a parent and child or between siblings. Sometimes a young child or teen may be struggling with a problem, and the parents turn to a therapist to diagnose it and come up with ways to address it.

Esther Boykin, a licensed marriage and family therapist in Washington, DC, says there is still some misunderstanding about what couples or family therapy is all about. In an interview on the *Girl with the Red Hair* blog, she says:

> Therapy is just a place to talk about what's not working in your life right now and figure out how to get through it. Whether it's something more serious like depression or trauma or something that seems more benign like marital conflict or getting through your kids' teenage years, a good therapist really can help. I hope that people will begin to see therapy as preventive instead of crisis control. We really have a lot to offer to everyone out there when it comes to living life to the fullest.

Issues that marriage and family therapists deal with include poor communication, child or adolescent behavior problems, substance abuse, infidelity, work stress, LGBTQ, infertility, grieving, and many other causes of marital or family discord. A therapist can work with couples who are dating, engaged, married, and divorced. Divorce counseling is especially important if there are children involved. Unlike a psychiatrist, who often looks for physical changes or abnormalities in the brain to treat a condition, a marriage and family therapist often focuses on the communication between members of a family and behaviors that can be modified.

A therapist usually begins by getting to know the couple or the family members. Once some background information is shared, the therapist will ask about any issues the family is dealing with. The therapist may ask, "What brought you here today?"—and the answers may be very different, depending on who is talking. Being able to get at the root of a problem when it is described in very different ways is an especially important skill for a marriage and family therapist. Teens may tell the therapist that their parents are always on their backs about schoolwork and being more responsible. The parents' version of that situation may be that they are simply encouraging their children to take their studies more seriously because they want them to be successful.

To understand what is really taking place within a family or couple's relationship, a good therapist will carefully observe how the

During a counseling session a young woman talks with a therapist about how she and her husband communicate with each other. Marriage and family therapists work with individuals, couples, and families on a range of issues that cause discord.

individuals interact with each other. Marriage and family therapist Darren Adamson says on the Careers in Psychology website that family dynamics is one of the most interesting parts of the job. He explains:

> The most compelling aspect of MFT is the focus on the whole system rather than on the individual. Intuitively it makes sense that intervening with as many members of a family system is much more effective than focusing efforts on only one person. Interaction among people affects all involved in a circular way. . . . In the 26 years of my practice it has been shown time and time again to be the best approach to doing therapy. Even though I do see individuals, I always am thinking in systems. My interventions are designed to impact as much of the systemic patterns as possible, even when I am only seeing one member of that system.

Therapists can recognize relationship problems and come up with strategies for their patients. This often includes substituting unhealthy behaviors with healthy ones or changing the words that are used when family members share their feelings or concerns. Sometimes therapy leads to the diagnosis of a condition such as depression or ADHD. This may lead a therapist to refer a patient to another mental health professional who specializes in that type of problem.

Some types of therapy are ongoing, such as for patients dealing with chronic conditions like bipolar disorder. MFT is sometimes meant to have a resolution; a problem is identified and then overcome. However, in many cases the goal of MFT is to help patients develop healthier or more productive ways of dealing with their challenges. The typical marriage and family therapist averages twelve sessions with a patient or family, with two-thirds of cases wrapped up within twenty sessions, according to the American Association for Marriage and Family Therapy (AAMFT). The AAMFT also reports that couples therapy usually resolves in twelve sessions, while child or adolescent cases take an average of nine sessions. When a therapist is working with only one member of a couple or family, cases usually take at least thirteen sessions.

How Do You Become a Marriage and Family Therapist?

Education

The path to becoming a marriage and family therapist usually starts with a bachelor's degree in psychology, social work, education, or a related field. A master's degree or doctorate in psychology or counseling is required in order to obtain a license to practice as a marriage and family therapist. Some universities offer graduate or PhD degrees specifically in MFT.

Certification and Licensing

Each state's requirements to become a licensed marriage and family therapist (LMFT) are a little different. Usually, a therapist needs between two thousand and four thousand hours of supervised clinical experience in order to obtain a state license. The licensing process also includes an exam and continuing education courses. An alternative to a state licensing exam is an exam administered by the Association of Marital and Family Therapy Regulatory Boards. Passing this exam can be used to meet licensing requirements in most states.

Volunteer Work and Internships

Many community-based agencies that assist children and families can use volunteers. These may include crisis centers, youth after-school programs, and other social service programs. Many of these agencies employ LMFTs. Volunteering with them can provide experience in helping families, as well as exposure to LMFTs and the opportunity to learn more about what their jobs entail.

Internships are essential in accruing the hours needed to meet graduate or doctoral degree requirements, as well as the requirements for a state license. Internships may be arranged through a university or by doing a job search online. MFT internships are available in hospitals, mental health clinics, local government public health offices, nonprofit agencies that serve families, and various charitable organizations.

Skills and Personality

A marriage and family therapist must be observant, a good listener, a problem solver, and have a personality that puts people at ease. Success in the job depends on getting often reluctant couples and kids to talk about their feelings, so being warm yet professional is very helpful. "I feel like when people open up to me, it is a gift that I don't treat lightly," California family therapist Lia Huynh said in an interview on the Careers in Psychology website. "And when I see them get better or make progress, I feel privileged that I got to be a part of that. It's such a rewarding experience."

Other important qualities include the ability to listen without judging, remain neutral when hearing different sides of the same problem, and separate oneself from one's patients. Therapist Esther Boykin says on the *Girl with the Red Hair* blog:

It's tough when I work with people who I can see are not ready to do the work to make changes—it's always heartbreaking to watch people stand in the way of the goals they have for themselves. It's also a humble reminder that no matter how much I know or how good of a therapist I try to be, in the end everyone is responsible for their own lives, and even I can't make them change.

On the Job

Employers

Most marriage and family therapists work as part of a larger practice of therapists, psychologists, or other mental health professionals, or they are in business for themselves. These therapists are also employed with government or nonprofit social service organizations, sometimes working alongside licensed clinical social workers, nurses, and other mental or physical health care providers.

Working Conditions

Most marriage and family therapists work in a comfortable office setting. Sometimes, though, the work is done at a family crisis center or a hospital. Occasionally, they may meet with parents and kids in a school. These therapists may hold workshops in meeting rooms or auditoriums in their communities. Because therapists usually work with students and working people, evenings and weekends are usually required to accommodate patients' schedules. This can make for long days. Also, therapists who own their own practices must often handle responsibilities such as accounting, marketing, billing, and the other aspects of a running a business.

Earnings

The median salary for a marriage and family therapist was $48,000 in 2016, according to the Bureau of Labor Statistics. The pay range is between $31,000 and $82,000 annually, though some therapists who own their own practice can make much more. The salary of these therapists depends on the cost of living in the region where they live, as well as their education, experience, and whether they are employed by a nonprofit, government, or private employer.

Opportunities for Advancement

A marriage and family therapist with a master's degree can make more money and take on more managerial roles by earning a doctorate. Work experience, however, is also critical to moving up, either within a private practice or in another setting. Like many careers in mental health, marriage and family therapists are needed everywhere. Career advancement may require moving to a new part of the country or simply to a different employer nearby.

What Is the Future Outlook for Marriage and Family Therapists?

There are about forty-eight thousand marriage and family therapists in the United States, according to the AAMFT. At any one time, about 1.8 million Americans are in couples or family therapy. The number of therapists needed across the country is growing, as is the number of people seeking therapy. As the stigma of mental health care continues to fade and people recognize the benefits of dealing openly with family issues, the outlook for marriage and family therapists is an encouraging one. As the baby boom generation ages, more work in this field will be done with older adults and a greater number of adults coping with the challenges that come with being parents and caring for their own parents.

Find Out More

American Association for Marriage and Family Therapy (AAMFT)
112 S. Alfred St.
Alexandria, VA 22314
website: www.aamft.org

The AAMFT helps educate the public about MFT and helps therapists in the field enhance their skills and knowledge. The organization also holds conferences and webinars and publishes a trade journal called *Family Therapy Magazine*.

International Association of Marriage and Family Counselors
website: www.iamfconline.org

This association offers credentialing and education to marriage and family therapists across the globe. The association's magazine, the *Family Journal*, publishes research, practice advice, and other relevant information for the benefit of students, educators, and working therapists.

International Family Therapy Association (IFTA)
Room 512 Safety Building
Rock Island, IL 61201
website: www.ifta-familytherapy.org

The IFTA holds conferences around the world to help improve the quality of family therapy. The association works with many other organizations to strengthen families and promote wellness.

National Board for Certified Counselors (NBCC)
3 Terrace Way
Greensboro, NC 27403
website: www.nbcc.org

The NBCC is a nonprofit, independent certification organization that promotes high standards in the counseling profession and the role of counselors and mental health in general. Its website offers certification information as well as career resources for substance abuse counselors and other types of counselors.

Substance Abuse Counselor

What Does a Substance Abuse Counselor Do?

At a Glance:
Substance Abuse Counselor

Minimum Educational Requirements

High school diploma

Personal Qualities

Patience, compassion, dedication, good communication skills

Certification and Licensing

Must obtain license or credential from the state

Working Conditions

Office setting at a rehab clinic, hospital, school, or correctional facility

Salary Range

About $26,000 to $63,000

Number of Jobs

As of 2015, about 94,000 in the United States

Future Job Outlook

Steady job growth, estimated to be 22 percent through 2024

Substance abuse counselors help people of all ages deal with alcohol or drug problems. Their goal is to help people overcome their addictions. Counselors work with people who may not accept that they have a substance abuse problem, or they have had so many drug- or alcohol-related problems that they desperately want help. It is a very challenging field of mental health care, but it is also experiencing considerable growth. The increase in prescription drug abuse in recent years has fueled a need for more trained professionals to help individuals in the grip of addiction. At the same time, passage of the Affordable Care Act means more services are available to help those who need drug and alcohol counseling.

Some substance abuse counselors work with individuals who have eating disorders or other unhealthy behavioral problems, but most focus on people who are addicted to or abuse drugs or alcohol. Their job is to help the individual learn ways to stay clean and sober. They do this by helping the user develop realistic goals. They also try to provide them with practical tools for meeting those goals. For example, individuals who turn to drugs to deal with stress would be counseled to find healthier ways to manage stress. Therapy might include helping them learn to meditate, develop exercise programs that they will stick with, or use cognitive behavioral therapy to change the thought patterns that result from stress.

A counselor meets with an individual in need of help and evaluates the health and substance abuse problem of the client. Then the counselor proposes a treatment plan that will include talk therapy or other interventions, depending on the client's situation. This is important because most users need realistic, practical strategies for staying clean if they are going to succeed with that objective. Family members may also be brought into the picture so they are aware of the strategies and goals being discussed in counseling.

The National Institute on Drug Abuse reports that the average successful case takes about forty sessions to complete. Many of the first sessions are designed to help build a client's trust in the counselor and to develop strategies that will keep a client coming back if the client is seeing a counselor on an outpatient basis. Preventing clients from dropping out early is a common challenge for all counselors. Clients may be in therapy because they were ordered there by a judge or pressured into it by relatives and friends. This makes it even more important that substance abuse counselors be able to connect quickly with their clients.

Substance abuse counselors also lead group therapy sessions. These sessions may include a patient's family and friends or be made up only of people who are working to overcome drug or alcohol abuse. Usually, a therapist tries to stay out of the conversation as much as possible to let others share their stories and feelings. Many group sessions center on a particular topic, such as coping with substance abuse triggers or mending damaged relationships with family members.

A substance abuse counselor may choose to specialize in working with a particular age group, with clients with specific addictions, or in a particular setting. Substance abuse counselors who work with teens may end up doing a lot of work in schools or in after-school programs. Some counselors specialize in crisis intervention. This is a situation in which a drug user is a threat to him- or herself or to someone else. Noncrisis intervention is counseling that is done when a drug or alcohol abuser seeks assistance or has friends or family members make arrangements to see a counselor.

Increasingly, the nature of substance abuse counseling is focusing on more than changing addiction behavior. Counselors are seeing how mental health intersects with substance abuse disorders. That means more counselors are broadening their skill set and knowledge base by getting more education. In an interview on the Addiction Hope website, certified addiction therapist Laura Simon-Sulzer said that this movement toward more research and study-based care makes substance abuse counseling even more fascinating.

> We are learning a lot from science. Every discovery, trial, study is a step ahead, an opportunity to help more efficiently. We now know that nearly 75% of alcoholics and addicts suffer from co-occurring mental disorders, such as depression, trauma, bi-polar disorder, anxiety, etc. The way we treat clients and patients has changed to adjust to this reality.

In addition to knowing more about how to apply mental health care concepts and strategies to the treatment of drug and alcohol abusers, counselors must take a holistic view of their clients and all their personal and professional needs. A substance abuse counselor often directs clients to resources that will help them land a job or get job training. A counselor needs to know where clients should go for assistance with welfare, housing, food, and legal aid, and he or she must be able to recognize when a client might need a psychiatrist or other physician.

Being a substance abuse counselor is a multifaceted job that is not without its challenges and potential setbacks. Addicts who appear to be on the right track often relapse and start using drugs again. Helping someone get clean can sometimes take years.

How Do You Become a Substance Abuse Counselor?

Education

Substance abuse counselors may have the greatest range of educational requirements of any mental health profession. A person with a high school diploma can enroll in a training program and receive certification from the National Certification Commission for Addiction Professionals under the auspices of the Association for Addiction Professionals (NAADAC). Level 1 certification requires three years or six thousand hours of supervised work as a counselor but no additional education. A counselor with a bachelor's degree or an advanced degree can get higher-level certification, which means that individual can take on more responsibility and have greater job opportunities and earnings potential. Some universities offer PhD programs in addiction psychology and related subjects, which would even further broaden a counselor's prospects.

Certification and Licensing

To work in private practice, a substance abuse counselor must be licensed by the state. This requires a master's degree and between two thousand and four thousand hours of supervised clinical experience, depending on the state. Passing a state exam is also required. To maintain a license, substance abuse counselors must participate in continuing education every year. Voluntary certification through organizations such as the NAADAC can enhance a counselor's qualifications and make that individual more appealing as a job candidate. Some employers may only hire counselors who are both licensed and certified.

Volunteer Work and Internships

Volunteering with organizations such as Alcoholics Anonymous, Narcotics Anonymous, or other community agencies that assist people with addictions can help someone decide whether this is a field he or she would like to pursue. Internships are available through local governments, hospitals, and universities for students and recent graduates. Internships are especially helpful for anyone seeking a master's degree and who needs to accrue the hours necessary to obtain a state license.

Skills and Personality

Being compassionate and encouraging are two important qualities every substance abuse counselor must possess. A counselor also needs a certain amount of toughness to help clients see the consequences of their behavior and to confront a client who may be making excuses or lying about using drugs or alcohol. Time management and the ability to work efficiently are also key skills, because many substance abuse counselors have heavy workloads.

Being able to work with a group and help facilitate conversation and the sharing of feelings and experiences are important skills for this type of counselor. Donna Mae Depola is a credentialed alcohol and substance abuse counselor who also runs a training center for would-be substance abuse counselors. In an interview on the Careers in Psychology website, she stressed the importance of being a positive, nonjudgmental communicator. "Being upbeat, friendly and engaging on a personal level helps me," she said. "I am able to help people because I meet them at their level and I don't judge them or get annoyed at them and I don't beat them up over relapse. What I do is not only counseling it is far greater than that. We have to be a mentor and advisor to our clients."

On the Job

Employers

Substance abuse counselors are employed by hospitals and residential and outpatient treatment clinics. They also work for government social service departments, correctional institutions, and schools. The highest percentage of counselors (22 percent) work in outpatient care centers, while another 20 percent work in residential facilities or substance abuse treatment centers, according to the Bureau of Labor Statistics.

Working Conditions

Unless they are employed at a drug rehab facility with a limited number of clients at any given time, most substance abuse counselors have heavy workloads with many clients. Work schedules often include nights and weekends. The risk of stress or burnout may be higher in this field than in some other areas of mental health. These clients may be more likely to miss appointments, not follow through on tasks discussed during sessions, and relapse after appearing to make progress. But the rewards of seeing a person turn his or her life around can be indescribable. "There are so many miracles in this field," Depola said in the Careers in Psychology article. "I try and concentrate on the successes we see and hope that the clients that are still using will come back and get help before it is too late."

Earnings

The median salary for a substance abuse counselor was $39,270 in 2016, according to the Bureau of Labor and Statistics. The pay range is between $26,000 and $63,000 annually. The more education and experience a counselor gains, the greater the income potential.

Opportunities for Advancement

While a high school diploma and NAADAC certification can get a person started as a professional substance abuse counselor, more education and training are necessary to advance. Universities across the country offer degrees focusing on substance abuse counseling and addiction psychology. Earning a master's degree in substance abuse counseling and working for two years in a supervised clinical setting meets most of the requirements to become certified by the National Board for Certified Counselors, a designation that makes a counselor more attractive to potential employers. Working in private practice probably affords the best chances to advance and earn more money.

What Is the Future Outlook for Substance Abuse Counselors?

There were about ninety-four thousand substance abuse counselors working in the United States in 2016. Job growth was expected to be at least 22 percent during the next decade. These jobs will be available in all parts of the country. Changes in insurance coverage mean more substance abuse treatment services will be available to more people in the years ahead. Also, the criminal justice system is changing, sending more drug offenders into treatment programs rather than correctional institutions. This means more states and communities will need to hire substance abuse counselors to work with offenders. Research has shown that individuals are less likely to get into legal trouble if they receive treatment for their drug problems.

Find Out More

American Society of Addiction Medicine (ASAM)
website: www.asam.org

The ASAM represents doctors, counselors, and other professionals involved in the treatment of people with drug and alcohol problems. It is an excellent resource for anyone looking to find out more about the types of careers related to addiction medicine.

Association for Addiction Professionals (NAADAC)
44 Canal Center Plaza, Suite 301
Alexandria, VA 22314
website: www.naadac.org

The NAADAC provides support, education, and advocacy for substance abuse counselors and those in related fields. The organization, through the National Certification Commission for Addiction Professionals, also certifies counselors who have met high standards of education and work experience.

National Association of Addiction Treatment Providers (NAATP)
website: www.naatp.org

The NAATP provides information about the latest treatments and research, as well as laws and policies that affect the industry. Its website has local and national career information. The NAATP also sponsors training programs for counselors who want to enhance their skills and knowledge.

National Board for Certified Counselors (NBCC)
3 Terrace Way
Greensboro, NC 27403
website: www.nbcc.org

The NBCC is a nonprofit, independent certification organization that promotes high standards in the counseling profession and the role of counselors and mental health in general. Its website offers certification information as well as career resources for substance abuse counselors and other types of counselors.

Licensed Clinical Social Worker

What Does a Licensed Clinical Social Worker Do?

A social worker helps people with the challenges of living, such as obtaining welfare or accessing social services, finding child care, securing job training, and juggling monthly bills. The job is all about helping people improve their lives by giving them the tools and information to get through their daily challenges. Similarly, a licensed clinical social worker (LCSW) is also dedicated to improving the lives of his or her clients. But these types of social workers do so by diagnosing and treating mental, emotional, and behavioral problems. An LCSW is a unique mental health professional because the job can touch on so many areas of concern: mental health, physical health, poverty, unemployment, domestic violence, education problems, drug and alcohol abuse, divorce, criminal justice, and more.

An LCSW usually meets with an individual client or a family at some of the worst times in their lives. They may have been evicted from their home. Drug addiction may be keeping someone from holding a job. A teenager may be at risk of dropping out of school and getting into serious legal trouble. An LCSW steps into these real-life situations and tries to help people pick up the pieces and get to a better place. Sometimes, the clients are grateful for the help and enthusiastic about changing their lives. Other times, real-life solutions do not comes as easily as they do in the examples taught in college classrooms, explained LCSW Nikelle Rosier-Butler on the All Psychology Schools website. "Change isn't as easy as they make it out to be in the books," she said. "Case examples we learn in school are easy, but real life is messy, and we have to be persistent in making social change. We have to respect our client's choices if they choose not to change."

The type of work LCSWs do depends on their employers and if they specialize in a particular area of social work. An LCSW specializing in geriatric care and working in a long-term residential facility works with the same residents, monitoring their mental health while making sure their other day-to-day needs are being met. But an LCSW working at a substance abuse clinic might see many new clients every week, while maintaining a case file of longer-term clients.

In addition to geriatric and substance abuse specialties, other areas of social work include those working primarily with children, families, schools, and the criminal justice system. The children are often from disadvantaged backgrounds and may be struggling with learning disabilities, behavior problems, or developmental delays; living in foster care; or facing other challenges. Family social work can involve working with people of all ages, helping parents who are estranged from their children or helping immigrant families adjust to life in the United States. LCSWs affiliated with schools often work with individual students and their families but may also organize programs aimed at improving the quality of life for students at the school. This might include programs to fight bullying or educate students about sexually transmitted diseases. An LCSW who works with criminal offenders will try to change the criminal behavior while also assisting clients with the other things they need to stay out of the court system.

While the scope of work can vary tremendously from one social worker to another, or even from one day to the next for the same social worker, there is at least one common element most LCSWs share: They almost always work closely with others in providing care for their clients. The team could include other social workers, parole officers, teachers, school counselors, physicians, nurses, and other mental health professionals such as psychiatrists.

While a traditional social worker is often focused on the external issues facing families, such as finances and housing, an LCSW is able to spend time counseling clients and coming up with strategies that will improve a client's behavior and outlook on life. In an interview on the Careers in Psychology website, LCSW Judi Cinéas described the rewards of counseling people who are often at rock bottom:

> As a counselor, you aren't just fixing some problems here and there, you are really helping people make a complete change in their life and you get to feel like you are really making a difference. I feel like I have always had that problem-solving gene and I have always been good at helping people work towards finding a solution to a problem, so when I am able to help people find that solution, it is especially gratifying.

The contributions of an LCSW extend far beyond an individual or family. Communities benefit from the work of LCSWs by having higher high school graduation rates, lower juvenile crime rates, reduced domestic violence rates, more efficient social service agencies, improved morale among teachers and students, and other positive impacts, according to a 2016 report from the National Association of Social Workers.

How Do You Become a Licensed Clinical Social Worker?

Education

Unlike a social worker, who can work without a master's degree, an LCSW needs a master's degree in order to obtain that license. A bachelor's degree in psychology, social work, or a similar subject is usually a good start. A master's degree in social work or in counseling usually takes two years beyond a bachelor's degree. It is also possible to get a PhD in social work.

Certification and Licensing

Each state has its own licensing requirements. Usually, though, a master's degree and two years of supervised clinical work is required to obtain a license. In some cases local governments will allow an individual to work as a clinical social worker without a license. The mental health care aspect of the job is much like what an LCSW would do, but because of the demand on local governments, some exceptions are made. An LCSW may also get certification from an independent, nonprofit organization such as the Council on Social Work Education.

Volunteer Work and Internships

Most two-year supervised internships following graduate school are paid. Many licensing boards are very exacting in what they want to see from someone seeking to become an LCSW. Applicants need to provide their college transcripts, three or more letters of recommendation from LCSWs and other mental health professionals they have worked with, and extensive documentation about the hours they have spent working with clients in a supervised setting. This supervised training may be under a more experienced LCSW or in some cases with a psychologist or psychiatrist. Getting a particular state's licensing requirements ahead of time is a wise move.

Skills and Personality

Goal setting and organization are two qualities every LCSW needs. From the moment an LCSW starts working with a client, he or she starts identifying the mental disorder if there is one, assessing all the needs of the client, and developing a plan to treat any mental health issues while also setting the client on a path toward self-sufficiency. Good communication skills are vital, too, so that the client fully understands the goal and how to get there. Another important skill is being able to set boundaries. The stories LCSWs hear and the struggles they see firsthand can be overwhelming at times. The desire to do too much or get too personally involved in helping clients can be a strong one. But to avoid burnout and maintain professionalism, boundaries have to be set and respected.

On the Job

Employers

Many LCSWs are employed by medical or mental health facilities. These can be traditional hospitals, psychiatric hospitals and other mental health facilities, veteran care centers, nursing homes, substance abuse rehabilitation centers, and community health agencies. An LCSW may also find employment at an individual school or in a school district. Juvenile justice centers and adult correctional facilities also hire LCSWs. These types of social workers also work at homeless shelters, domestic abuse crisis centers, and nonprofit agencies that assist families in need. Local governments and child welfare departments also hire LCSWs.

Working Conditions

An LCSW can work in any number of settings, from long-term residential facilities to homeless shelters and from rural schools in high-poverty areas to large, metropolitan-area hospitals. The conditions, though, will always be challenging, as an LCSW is usually dealing with clients who have multiple issues in their lives. These people have been through a lot, whether it is losing a home, a loved one, or a job. They are at a point in their lives that they do not have a lot of control, whether because of dementia, addiction, or overwhelming financial problems. A parent may find that a child is dealing with a mental disorder that the parent is not equipped to handle. The conditions can be stressful, but an LCSW usually has other people and resources to help out. Maintaining a support group of other professionals is important.

Earnings

According to the Bureau of Labor Statistics, the median pay for an LCSW in 2016 was about $53,000. The range was between $28,500 and $77,000. The wide range is due to the type of employer and the cost of living in the community in which an LCSW resides. Working for a nonprofit agency or for a local government in a rural community is not going to bring in the same salary as working for a private hospital in a large metropolitan area.

Opportunities for Advancement

An LCSW with years of experience can move up into a managerial role, supervising other social workers at a health care agency or other employer. Obtaining a doctorate can also enhance the opportunities for advancement or allow a person to teach social work and counseling courses at the college or university level. Also, an LCSW who is passionate about the counseling aspect of the job may be able to take courses and move into another mental health field, such as marriage and family therapy.

What Is the Future Outlook for Licensed Clinical Social Workers?

Growth in this field is expected to be about 12 percent through 2024, but there is no reason to think that it will slow down after that. There will always be a need for LCSWs. Problems are unavoidable in life, and if someone is dealing with life's everyday problems while also struggling with a mental or behavioral issue, a dedicated LCSW can be just the person to help turn things around.

Find Out More

American Association for Marriage and Family Therapy (AAMFT)
112 S. Alfred St.
Alexandria, VA 22314
website: www.aamft.org

The AAMFT helps educate the public about marriage and family therapy and helps therapists in the field enhance their skills and knowledge. The organization also holds conferences and webinars and publishes a trade journal called *Family Therapy Magazine*.

Clinical Social Work Association
PO Box 10
Garrisonville, VA 22463
website: www.clinicalsocialworkassociation.org

This association works to advance the role of licensed clinical social work in the field of mental health care. It also acts a resource for LCSWs to learn more about policies and laws that affect their work.

Council on Social Work Education (CSWE)
1701 Duke St., Suite 200
Alexandria, VA 22314
website: www.cswe.org

The CSWE is an association of social work education programs that share information and work together to improve the quality of training for social work students and current practitioners. The council also grants accreditation to licensed clinical social workers who participate in continuing education.

National Association of Social Workers (NASW)
750 First St. NE, Suite 800
Washington, DC 20002
website: www.socialworkers.org

The NASW supports the professional growth of all types of social workers and works to maintain high standards in the field. The association publishes five professional journals and offers a variety of continuing education programs.

National Board for Certified Counselors (NBCC)
3 Terrace Way
Greensboro, NC 27403
website: www.nbcc.org

The NBCC is a nonprofit, independent certification organization that promotes high standards in the counseling profession and the role of counselors and mental health in general. Its website offers certification information as well as career resources for substance abuse counselors and other types of counselors.

Interview with a Licensed Mental Health Counselor

Miriam Lacher is a licensed mental health counselor at Sarasota Memorial Hospital in Florida. She has worked as a counselor for thirty years. She spoke with the author about her career.

Q: Why did you become a mental health counselor?

A: It was sort of by chance, but it's been incredibly rewarding. I had been a teacher in New Jersey, teaching adults, which I enjoyed very much. I moved to Florida and couldn't really find a good fit teaching. A friend had written some books about psychology and counseling and I was fascinated. I got my second master's degree, this one in rehabilitation counseling. Some people with that degree go into social work or helping people with disabilities. But I chose mental health counseling. Sarasota Memorial Hospital had started a drug and alcohol rehabilitation program, which I became very interested in. I love working with that population, so I've stayed with it for thirty years.

Q: Can you describe your typical workday?

A: Every day is different, which is one of the things I love about this job. A typical day might include some one-on-one counseling with patients. We'll focus on what's working and what's not working in their lives. There's also a lot of group therapy sessions throughout the week. I work with nurses, too, educating them about the challenges and rewards of working with these types of patients. Part of my day often includes consulting with other counselors, nurses and doctors about particular patients. And, of course, there's always a lot of paperwork. You have to keep detailed records of each case. It's important, but it's time consuming, and it takes time away from working with people and their families.

Q: What do you like most and least about your job?

A: Watching people change their lives so dramatically has been a tremendous emotional payoff for me. The work you do makes such a big difference for not only the individual, but their family, too. You get to watch family dynamics change in a positive way. It's amazing. The other thing is that I've been fortunate to work in a hospital where I could always hear other points of view. I like the idea that I'm in a hospital with all these brilliant psychiatrists. Being part of an institution like this has afforded me opportunities I don't think I would have had in private practice. I get to do a lot of community outreach and organizing programs at the hospital. I never would have thought about doing that sort of thing when I started.

Sometimes working in an institution means things move very slowly. There can be a lot of bureaucracy. I'm disappointed that some things take so long at the hospital.

Q: What personal qualities do you find most valuable for this type of work?

A: Listening and hearing are at the top of the list. It's important to listen, but I need to really hear what you're saying and what you're not saying. If you don't like listening to people's stories, and if you're not interested in the human condition, this probably isn't the career for you. People want to tell their stories. You have to be compassionate, but you do need to have a strong spine, too. It can be a challenging job, but someone has to speak up for those who can't always speak up for themselves. You also need to know your strengths and weaknesses. You have to be willing to say, "I need to refer you to someone else. You're dealing with something that might be better handled by a specialist in this area."

Q: What advice do you have for students who might be interested in this career?

A: Know what your reason is for wanting this type of career. Ask yourself, "Why do I want to do this?" It's easy to imagine how something is going to be. That can take you down a path that may or may not be what you envisioned. You should always make decisions based on good information. Go to people who have experience in whatever field you're interested in and ask them about the job—what they like about it, what they don't. Find out as much as you can about what a job entails. You also have to understand the amount of education you need for a job. Once you've done your research, you'll have a much better idea if this career is right for you.

Other Careers in Mental Health

Art therapist
Biogerontologist
Career counselor
Child abuse counselor
Child psychologist
Cognitive neuroscientist
Cognitive psychologist
Community mental health
    counselor
Community psychologist
Consumer psychologist
Depression counselor
Development psychologist
Domestic violence counselor
Engineering psychologist
Environmental psychologist
Forensic psychologist
Gerontologist

Grief counselor
Licensed mental health
    counselor
Life coach
Media psychologist
Mental health clinician
Military psychologist
Multicultural counselor
Music therapist
Neuropsychologist
Organizational/industrial
    psychologist
Pastoral counselor
Rehabilitation psychologist
School guidance counselor
School social worker
Suicide intervention counselor
Veterans' counselor

Editor's Note: The US Department of Labor's Bureau of Labor Statistics provides information about hundreds of occupations. The agency's *Occupational Outlook Handbook* describes what these jobs entail, the work environment, education and skill requirements, pay, future outlook, and more. The *Occupational Outlook Handbook* may be accessed online at www.bls.gov/ooh.

Index

Picture Credits

About the Author

James Roland started out as a newspaper reporter more than twenty-five years ago and then moved on to become an editor, magazine writer, and author.